ESSENTIAL 

INVES
BASICS

ADAM SHAW
AND
MARC ROBINSON

LONDON, NEW YORK, MUNICH,
MELBOURNE, DELHI

Project Editor Richard Gilbert
Senior Art Editor Sarah Cowley

DTP Designer Rajen Shah
Production Controller Sarah Sherlock

Managing Editor Adèle Hayward
Managing Art Editor Marianne Markham
Category Publisher Stephanie Jackson

Produced for Dorling Kindersley by
PORTAL PUBLISHING
43 Stanley Street, Brighton
East Sussex BN2 0GP

Creative Director Caroline Marklew
Editorial Director Lorraine Turner

First published in Great Britain in 2003
by Dorling Kindersley Limited,
80 Strand, London WC2R 0RL

A Penguin company

2 4 6 8 10 9 7 5 3 1

Copyright © 2003
Dorling Kindersley Limited, London

Text copyright © 2003
Adam Shaw and Marc Robinson

All rights reserved. No part of this publication may be reproduced, stored in a retrieval system, or transmitted in any form or by any means, electronic, mechanical, photocopying, recording, or otherwise, without the prior permission of the copyright owner.

A CIP catalogue record for this book is available from the British Library

ISBN 0 7513 3725 0

Reproduced by Colourscan, Singapore
Printed in Hong Kong by Wing King Tong

See our complete catalogue at
www.dk.com

CONTENTS

Exploring Financial Risk

Finding Ways to Manage Risk

Understanding Performance

Starting Out with Confidence

INTRODUCTION

Putting your money into investments can be one of the most financially rewarding activities you do, or it can be one of the most unnerving. So much of investing is tied to our hopes and dreams, inhibitions and fears, that it can be difficult separating the real from the imagined risks. The fact that the world of investing can itself be overwhelming drives many people from participating at all. Investing Basics *is designed to help you grasp easily the relatively few basic elements that form the foundation of everything in investing. From this book, you will gain a clear understanding of setting goals, developing strategies, selecting the most appropriate investments, handling risks intelligently, using time wisely, and finding professionals to help when you need them. Most of all,* Investing Basics *will give you the confidence to be in control of your money as you aim towards a stable, comfortable future.*

CONTROLLING YOUR MONEY

The most important rule of investing is so simple, it is easy to take it lightly: you decide what will happen with your money. What it can do for you is up to you.

DECIDING WHAT TO DO

The moment you receive money, you have to use it. Whether you decide to spend it, keep it close by, bank it, or trust others to borrow it, you always have something to gain or lose. Here are the main choices.

You should understand what you are getting in return for giving up control of your money.

SPENDING MONEY

You can buy things with it (always the crowd favourite).

KEEPING MONEY AT HOME

If you store money at home, it will be available for you to use at any time. However, it is a sure way to lose money because inflation will slowly erode its buying power.

BANKING MONEY

You can lend money to banks. By opening an account, you lend it to them until you need it. In return, you can have cheques for quick access to your money and earn interest from a savings account or similar investment.

LENDING MONEY

You can lend money by buying bonds (where the bond issuer repays lenders like you with interest). Governments and companies borrow money for many reasons, for example to carry out improvements and for research and development.

2

Investing your money should be about investing for a better life – for you to enjoy or for a loved one.

BUYING PUBLICLY OWNED COMPANIES

You can become a part-owner of a company by buying some of its shares. If the company does well, you might participate in the success. If it does poorly, you may lose money just as any company owner would. Over time, you hope that the value of the shares you hold will rise, but you must expect some ups and downs.

USING FUND MANAGERS

You can also select a pooled investment fund run by a professional manager. You select the fund that specializes in the type of investment you like and then leave it to the manager to decide which shares to buy and sell.

INVESTING IN BRICKS AND MORTAR

You can buy a home or other property. You gain or lose according to how the property value fluctuates.

TAKING A GAMBLE

You can bet on a roll of the dice, buy lottery tickets, do the pools, or play any game of chance and hope to make a profit – or risk losing it all. You could also invest your money in shares and bonds without knowing what you are doing – this would be just as much of a gamble.

USING BASIC PRINCIPLES

To invest means to use something in a way that will give you more value in the future. Deciding to invest means thinking of your time and money as tools for achieving some worthwhile goals.

UNDERSTANDING SECURITIES

A security is the generic name used for any type of financial instrument that can be bought and sold. The two main types of securities are shares and bonds. The owner of a share is a part-owner in a business. The shareholder benefits from the performance of the business by hoping for a rise in the price of the share and by receiving a flow of dividends. The owner of a bond is a lender to a business or government. Just because these financial instruments are called securities does not mean that they are secure. Both bonds and shares can lose money as well as make money.

MAKING MONEY WORK FOR YOU

If you owned a company, you would have employees working for you. Think of your money that way. The more money you send out in the world to work for you, the more money you can accumulate to produce wealth for you.

EXPLORING YOUR INVESTMENT CHOICES

As an investor, your job is to find opportunities to use (invest) your money. For example, you can:

- Be a lender or an owner.
- Keep the money close to you or let others use it for longer periods with more control.

The longer you let someone use your money, the more you should be paid for that use. The more risk people put your money under, the more they should be willing to pay you for trusting them with those risks.

BUYING LOW, SELLING HIGH

Usually you cannot tell when an investment is highly priced and ready for a fall, or vice versa. However, you can keep in mind the following points:

- Professionals often recognize a high price and sell a security before the general public reaches the same conclusion, leaving average investors as the ones to carry the losses.
- The higher the price goes, the more people become fearful and begin to sell.
- People tend to look at past performance instead of future prospects, and therefore often end up buying high and selling low.
- It is more difficult for something to rise than for it to fall, which means that prices are generally capable of falling much faster than they rise.

3 Investing is a matter of deciding how much trust or faith you have in the promises that are being made to you.

GUARDING YOUR MONEY FROM LOSSES

It is a lot easier to lose money than it is to make more. For example, percentages are misleading. If you lose 50% of your money, it will then take a 100% gain, not a 50% gain, to get you back to where you started. For this reason, you must always do plenty of research before you invest your money.

DEFINING SAVING

Over a lifetime, people often become wealthy because they follow these two simple rules. First, they save, meaning that they spend less than they earn. Second, they use credit wisely and do not become overextended in debt.

PREPARING YOURSELF FOR WEALTH

A financial plan does not have to be perfect. You can always adjust it as you learn. Every goal – and every plan to achieve that goal – is as individual as the person who makes it.

DEFINING YOUR GOALS

It is important to set clear goals for how you want to use your money. A goal is what you want to achieve in your life. The money you accumulate will help you get there.

For example, your goal could be a house, a car, college education for your children, a comfortable retirement, an amount of money by a certain date, or an income stream for your family when you die or if you cannot work. It could be food for the local shelter every Christmas for the next ten years, or a donation to help find a cure for a disease.

Setting goals helps you give the concept of investing some shape and definition. They help to give a sense of how much money you will need, and how much time you have before you will need it.

PLANNING YOUR STRATEGY

Set your strategy according to what you want to accomplish.

Protection. Do you want to protect what you already have saved? For example, if you have saved enough for a deposit on a home, you will need to invest it in something safe until you find the right home.

Income. Do you want to earn income? Maybe you need just enough money to be able to afford a small holiday without spending the savings you already have, or to make some home improvements.

Growth. Do you need to accumulate a large amount of money to be able to pay for a major goal in your life? Exactly how much, for example, would you like to be able to contribute to your child's education at college?

4 Every investment plan focuses on goals, strategy, investment type, and risk.

CHOOSING THE RIGHT INVESTMENTS

By now you will have gauged how much money you will need, and how much time you have to reach your goal. Maybe you need to earn a lot in a short time, or you may need to earn an amount that seems appropriate for the amount of time you have available. You might even be lucky enough to have plenty of time to achieve your goal. With this awareness, you can narrow the field of possible investments by identifying which ones have at least the potential to achieve your goal within your time frame.

5 Time plays a critical role in every investment decision. Consider it carefully.

IDENTIFYING RISK LEVELS

Once you have assessed your goals, understood the basic strategies, and looked at what investments might get you there on time, you can look at the more predictable outcomes of investments and the potential risks from a more analytical, rather than emotional, perspective.

For example, you may decide that the risk of losing some money is relatively minor compared to the risk of not reaching your goal. If, on the other hand, the risk of a particular investment seems too high, you will have to consider how far short of your goal you would be willing to fall. When you have defined your priorities, you can explore whether other investments, or combinations of investments, might offer a more acceptable level of risk.

WORKING WITH STRATEGIES

While investment strategies have a reputation for being quite complex, the cornerstone strategies are simple, and most are used by even the most advanced investors.

TAKING THE BASIC STEPS

You buy. You hold. You sell. These three basic steps are what it takes to be an investor; the fundamental elements of every investment strategy.

HOLDING ON TO YOUR INVESTMENTS

How long you hold an investment can affect every other aspect of your strategy. For example, if your strategy is protection, you would choose an investment with the best potential safety during your planned holding period. For an income strategy, you would look for an investment that can provide the income you need during your holding period. For a growth strategy, you would look for an investment with the potential to rise in price in accordance with your time frame.

6 The most basic decision – whether to hold or to sell – may also be the most difficult.

7 You will see that investment analysts often recommend securities as a "buy", a "hold", or a "sell".

TIMING THE MARKET OR INVESTING FOR THE LONG TERM?

Time, not timing, is often the best help when it comes to investing in the stock market. If you jump in and out of the market, you might time it correctly. On the other hand, you might miss the best returns. For example, if you had invested £1,000 from 1935 to the year 2002, here is how your money could have performed:

INVESTMENT PERIOD (1 JULY 1935 TO 30 JUNE 2002)	TOTAL VALUE
If you invested for all 17,000 days:	£65,452
If you missed the 10 best days:	£33,458
If you missed the 100 best days:	£ 1,461

** Source: stock market historian David Schwartz*

EMOTIONAL SELLING AND DAY TRADING

Some investors trade on emotions or try to beat the market through quick trades for profits. Day trading can be very risky and involves speculating rather than investing. Trying to profit from a number of quick trades is even harder because you have to overcome the continual commissions you have to pay to the brokers to buy and sell on your behalf.

HOLDING SHORT-TERM: TRADING

Short-term trading involves *timing the market*, where you buy low and sell high soon after. Successful trading takes a lot of close attention, courage, and luck. It may also work out to be expensive, because you will probably have to pay a fee every time you trade and you may also have to pay capital gains taxes if you make a profit.

In order to illustrate this, if you pay 5% commission to sell a security, earn 8% profit, then sell, you would have only 3% left. Likewise, if you buy 100 shares at £10 each (total £1,000) and pay £35 in commission (3.5%), the price of your shares would have to go up by 3.5% just to break even.

HOLDING LONG-TERM: INVESTING

If you take a longer-term approach – if your goals are bigger and more far-reaching – there is probably no need to buy and sell quickly. You can find a use for your money that coincides with your longer-term goals, then give it time to do what you expect it to do without worrying whether the price falls occasionally. This is the strategy most financial professionals recommend, particularly for people who want their money to grow over time. It will help cushion your investments from the effects of short-term fluctuations in the stock market.

USING THE THREE MAIN STRATEGIES

Being a successful investor does not necessarily mean making a lot of money. Like choosing the proper clothes for the occasion, the right strategy is the one that suits your goal. Whether you are rich or poor, a beginner or an expert, there are three basic investment strategies.

PROTECTING YOUR MONEY

One strategy is simply to hold on to what you have already saved. This means safety is your top priority. However, safety does not translate into a do-nothing approach. On the contrary, doing nothing with money or keeping it in a no-interest account allows inflation to erode its buying power until it has less value than when you started. For protection, therefore, investors try to keep close control over their money by lending it for short periods to borrowers who have reliable reputations.

Since borrowers cannot do much with money they have to repay quickly, they should not pay much interest. That is an acceptable trade-off for investors who consider an investment to be successful if it earns enough to offset inflation and protects their money until they need it. However, lending money even for short periods can be risky, so check the risks before you invest.

EARNING INCOME

The second main strategy is to make income the top priority. This means earning an income that will not only outpace inflation, but provide some additional money as well. Investing to earn income is for people who want to receive regular instalments of money, or who want at least some predictability in the amount they can earn or when they will earn it.

Investors with income as a main strategy allow others to use their money for longer periods of time than they would allow if they were simply protecting their money. In return, they expect to be better compensated for taking the added risk that is a by-product of having less control.

8 Be suspicious of any investment that is supposedly designed to meet all three basic strategies.

9 Many professionals believe asset allocation is the most critical factor in investment performance.

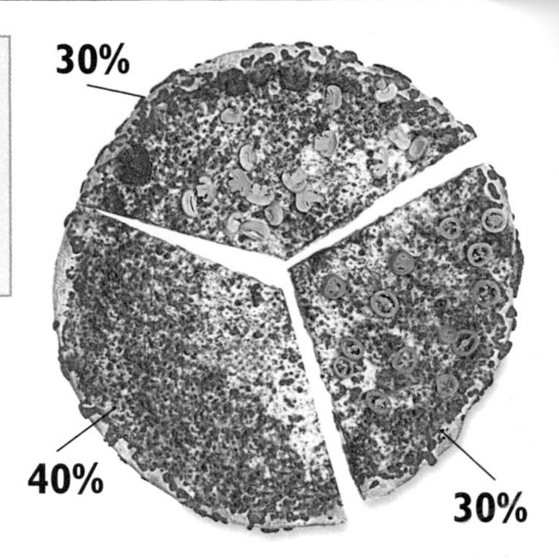

GROWING MORE

The third main strategy involves using your money to grow more money – even, in some cases, as much money as you can. A growth strategy requires investors to give up the most control over their money and a significant level of predictability about the success of the strategy.

In return for unpredictability and loss of control, growth investors expect to be more highly compensated than protection or income investors, and within a reasonable time period. If the compensation – in the form of a share price rise, for example – does not materialize, the investors can sell, although this would mean taking a loss on their investment.

▲ UNDERSTANDING ASSET ALLOCATION

There are three main asset classes that coincide with the three main investment strategies. Dividing or allocating the available money among the asset classes is considered a crucial part of any investment plan. Each asset class is better suited for a particular strategy than the other two. Investors typically allocate certain percentages of their investment money to each asset class. Cash equivalents is the asset class most used by investors with a protective strategy. Fixed income, typically bonds, is the asset class most used by investors with an income strategy. Equities, typically shares, is the asset class most used by investors with a growth strategy. Percentages for each class vary according to the goals of each investor, but one arrangement might be the 30%-30%-40% allocation model shown above. Others might place more emphasis on shares.

COMBINING STRATEGIES

Some investments are designed to meet two strategies. For example, balanced equity funds are designed both to generate income and to achieve growth. Like buying a sofa bed that is not as good as a bed or as good as a sofa, you may sacrifice some of one strategy's potential in exchange for having dual requirements.

GROWING MONEY IN THE TWO SIMPLEST WAYS

The simple act of not touching your money allows the easiest, most powerful strategy ever devised for making money – compounding – *to work its magic. It also helps you save on taxes. This is the most valuable lesson in investing: the more money you have, the faster it can grow. In other words, as money accumulates, the pace of its growth accelerates. It is natural to want to spend some of your profit. However, if you have a long time before you need the money, you may want to let it accumulate instead and grow faster as it does so. Here is how compounding works.*

USING THE POWER OF COMPOUNDING

It takes discipline to reinvest earnings instead of spending them. You will notice, however, that after a few years the strategy will pay off because the growth will accelerate faster than during the earlier years.

Keeping Your Hands off the Money
Say, for example, you start by investing £1,200 a year in an equity fund that earns 8% a year. Every year, you reinvest earnings so that they also earn 8% interest. After twenty years, you will have over £45,000 after tax.

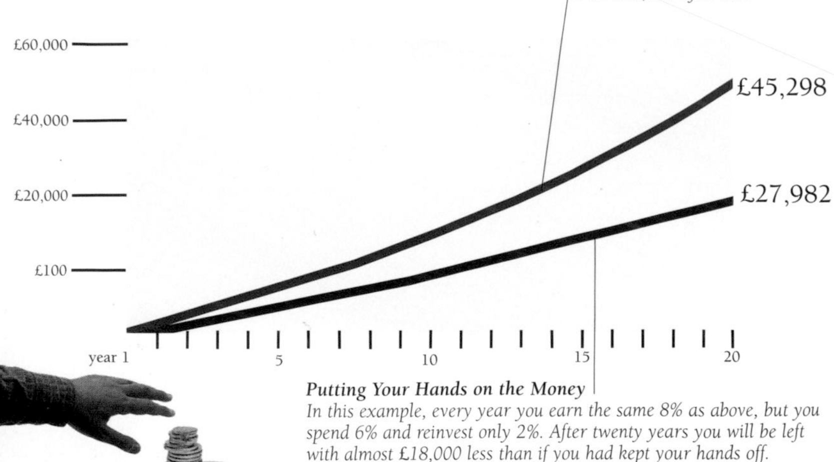

Putting Your Hands on the Money
In this example, every year you earn the same 8% as above, but you spend 6% and reinvest only 2%. After twenty years you will be left with almost £18,000 less than if you had kept your hands off.

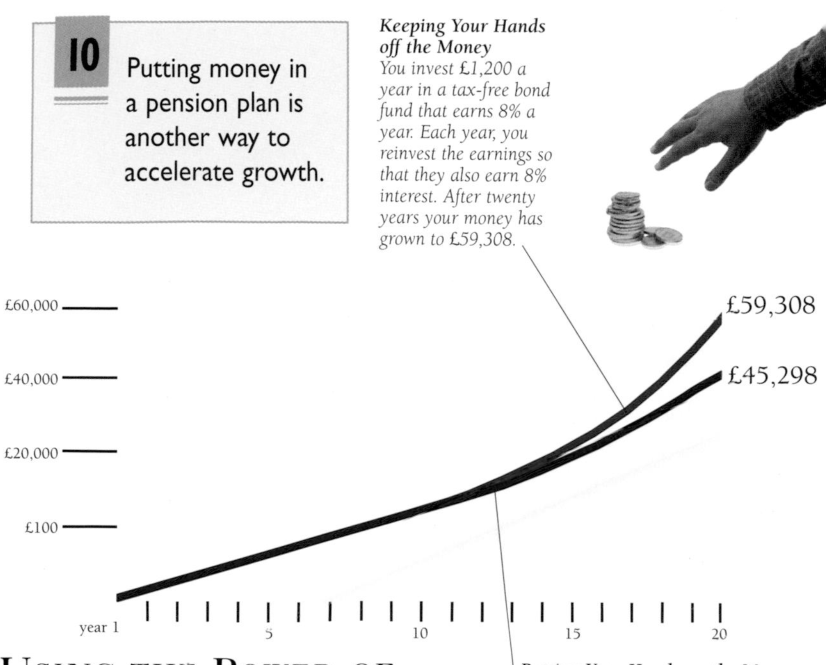

Keeping Your Hands off the Money
You invest £1,200 a year in a tax-free bond fund that earns 8% a year. Each year, you reinvest the earnings so that they also earn 8% interest. After twenty years your money has grown to £59,308.

Putting Your Hands on the Money
You invest the same £1,200 and earn the same 8% as above, but because you are not investing tax-deferred or tax-free, every year you pay tax on your earnings. After twenty years, you end up with just over £14,000 less than had you kept the Government's hands off.

USING THE POWER OF REDUCED TAXES

A major part of any plan to grow money involves reducing taxes. In fact, the Government encourages you to use your money in socially desirable ways by letting you skip paying taxes on some investments or by allowing you to receive gross interest on others. For example, although the income from gilts is not tax-free, it is paid before tax has been deducted, and gains are free of capital gains tax. Likewise, if you invest money in an ISA (Individual Savings Account), any profits you make will be free of tax. If reinvesting earnings makes money grow faster, reinvesting all your earnings – in short, avoiding taxes – will accelerate growth even more.

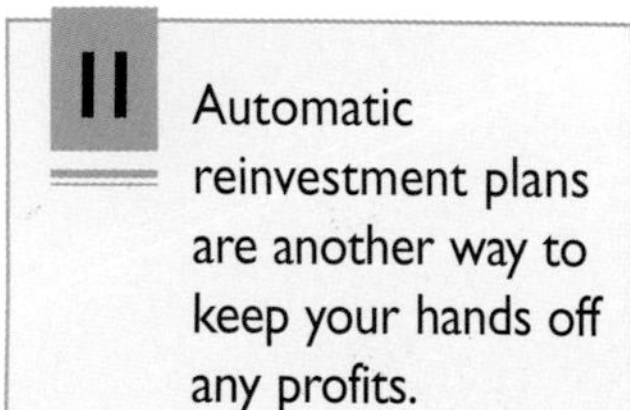

FINDING A MATCH FOR YOUR MONEY

Once you know your goals, you can look for investments that at least will give you a chance to reach those targets. Keep in mind that institutions trying to attract your money have different purposes. It is up to you to understand those purposes and to see whether they match your own. In short, you may want to match the promise of an investment with your own needs and look for compatibility. Here are a few choices to help you get started.

BUYING INTO SMALL COMPANIES

Small companies are usually looking to expand and grow. That may mean investing more in research and development, establishing a new product line, or other similar uses. Typically, they reinvest all their profits – if they have any – back into the business instead of distributing them to shareholders. People who buy shares in small companies are not looking for income. They believe that the companies will grow and make their shares more valuable over time.

INVESTING IN LARGE COMPANIES

Companies that have been around for a while tend to provide more stability by having established product lines. Some have products with consistent, dependable sales even in unfavourable economic climates. Many earn enough profits to pay a portion to their shareholders.

People who buy these kinds of shares are often looking for slow, steady increases in share prices, with the added benefit of a little extra income.

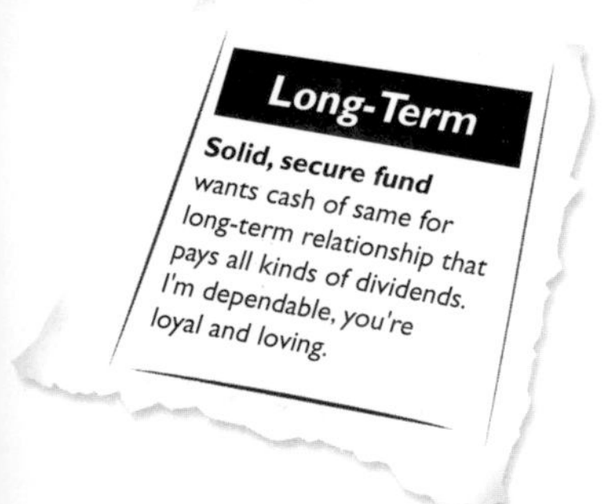

MAKING SHORT-TERM LOANS

Many companies and governments borrow money for specific periods to manage cash flow, cover operating costs, or meet other expenses. They will pay some interest and return your money at the end of the agreed period. The longer they keep it, the higher the interest rate you can expect them to pay.

There is always a risk that your loan will not be repaid. Some bonds therefore have a higher risk than others and are usually graded so that you have some idea of the risk attached to them.

MAKING INTERMEDIATE OR LONG-TERM LOANS

Many companies and government entities have long-term goals that require financing. For example, companies may need money for new plants, offices, or technologies. Governments may need to build roads or provide other community services. Typically, the longer they will want to use your money, the higher the interest they will be willing to pay to get the loan.

People who make longer-term loans usually want to secure a predictable income at higher rates than are available from making short-term loans.

13 Successful investing is dependent upon matching your investments with your goals.

12 Remember not to lock away money you may need in a hurry at some time in the future – always keep some in reserve.

MAKING HIGH-RISK LOANS

Some institutional borrowers have difficulty attracting lenders. They may possibly have a poor record of repaying other loans. Maybe the purpose of the loan is itself a high-risk venture. The money they borrow from investors may even go to pay off another loan. So to attract lenders, these borrowers must pay higher interest to make the potential income worth the risks. *Junk bonds* are one form of high-risk borrowing.

CHOOSING INVESTMENTS

Your investments reflect your decisions about how others can use your money. Be sure you can accept those uses. With that in mind, here are the main types of investments.

USING CASH EQUIVALENTS

Since one strategy is to protect what you have already saved, there are investments designed with safety as the top priority. When you invest in securities from an asset class called "cash equivalents", you are trying to protect your money and earn a little income at the same time.

UNDERSTANDING CASH EQUIVALENTS

Investing in cash equivalents lets you keep your money close and safe by lending it for very short periods (from a day to a year) to borrowers with reliable reputations. Investments designed for protection are called cash equivalents because, in practice, they are designed to be almost as safe as cash.

ASSESSING LIQUIDITY

The faster you can get your money from an investment, the more *liquid* it is considered to be.

USING CASH EQUIVALENTS

Many experts recommend keeping on hand at least six months' worth of income in an instant access savings account for emergency situations, such as losing a job. You may also choose to invest in cash equivalents if you are close to the time when you will be using the money. For example, you may have enough for a deposit on a home and do not want to risk losing it.

CHOOSING MONEY MARKET FUNDS

These funds are similar to savings accounts except that your money is pooled with other customers' money. It is then loaned to businesses for a short time, usually a week or less and sometimes overnight.

Money market funds are thought to be one of the safest investments. All the customers share the interest earned and the bank takes a small fee for its efforts. It is still possible to lose money, however, so before investing, you should ask in writing whether the fund is covered by an officially recognized investor compensation scheme and what credit rating the fund has from one of the major credit rating agencies.

USING SAVINGS AND CURRENT ACCOUNTS

When you put money into these types of account, you are in fact making loans to your bank with no time limits. You have the right to withdraw your money immediately or with a pre-agreed notice period. The bank lends your money to individuals or businesses and pays a portion of the interest it earns back to you. While you earn some income from a savings account, it is designed mainly to protect what you already have. The interest you earn is among the lowest of any investment and the income is usually taxable, reducing your income even further.

PUTTING MONEY INTO A CASH ISA

The term ISA stands for Individual Savings Account. Although there are different types of ISAs, the cash ISA is the most straightforward and least risky. It operates in a very similar way to most cash-based bank or building society accounts. However, like all bank and building society accounts, the rules differ depending on which organization you have chosen for investing your money. It is therefore very important to check the specific requirements and rules surrounding the account before you deposit any money. It is also important to understand that an ISA is only a wrapper. It protects your savings from tax. That is obviously a good thing, but an ISA is only as good as what is inside the wrapper. It is the same with chocolate. It is nice to have a great wrapper but it has got to taste good as well. In other words, if you are opening a cash ISA, make sure you are happy with the interest and details of the specific account as well as the tax-saving advantages.

14 Many investors use cash equivalents as temporary *parking places* until they are ready to use the money for something else.

LENDING MONEY: BONDS

When you buy fixed income securities, typically bonds, you are lending money to earn some income. The borrower might be a corporation or a government.

INVESTING IN BONDS

Bonds are the major alternative to a stock market investment. They can provide either income or capital growth, depending on whether you buy and hold, or speculate by buying low and selling high.

1. RAISING MONEY

Here is an example. A government needs to raise money to build, renovate, fund its operating costs, or simply to pay off other debts. It decides how much money it will need and how long it will need to repay the lenders (the investors). It also decides the lowest interest rate it could get away with paying while still attracting enough interest from investors. It will have to pay an agreed rate of interest for a fixed number of years. At the end of the agreed term, it will also have to pay back the original loan.

2. FLOATING AN OFFER

The investment banker floats an offer to the public (tests it) to see if it can sell enough bonds at the proposed terms in order to raise all the money. If it can, everything moves ahead. If it cannot, it may either reprice (decide a new interest rate and other terms) and try again, or withdraw the offer.

3. ACCEPTING THE OFFER

This is where you come in. Say you and other investors decide to invest. In effect, you are saying, "I'll lend you money. I'm willing to accept your promise to repay my loan plus interest, by the specific date, according to the terms in your offer". For example, you may buy several twenty-year bonds for £1,000 each. The corporation will be expected to pay a fixed interest rate of, say, 6% (£60) every year, in four annual instalments, for twenty years.

15 You can sell a bond at any time and take a profit or loss, apart from any interest you have earned.

4. PROFITING FROM FALLING INTEREST RATES

If interest rates drop, new bond issuers will enter the market selling new bonds with lower interest rates than yours. That will make your bonds more valuable. You could decide to sell your bonds. There will probably be others willing to buy. If you do sell, you can demand a profit (called a premium) because the bond pays more than the going rate. For example, if new bonds are being issued at 4%, buyers might agree to pay you £1,090 per bond for your 6% bonds. You would earn a £90 profit on each bond, and they would replace you as the new lenders. Now it would be their turn to receive interest payments and assume the risks of lending to this particular borrower.

5. ACTING ON RISING INTEREST RATES

If rates rise, the reverse of the above situation would occur. Your 6% bonds would be less valuable because investors could do better than 6% by buying new bonds. If the going rate for newly issued bonds is 8%, you may be forced to sell at a discount (for example, £920) to entice potential buyers. You would have earned the interest up to the point of selling, but you would also take a loss of £80 on the original investment. (The bond cost £1,000. You sold it for £920. The difference is £80.)

6. GETTING PAID: THE LOAN ENDS

After twenty years, time is up on the loan. Every owner of these bonds at this time is paid £1,000 for each one, no matter when they bought the bond or at what price. For example, the person who paid you £920 per bond would now receive £1,000, or an £80 profit per bond, in addition to the interest earned.

THINKING LIKE A LENDER

You may be "investing" in a bond, but you should still think like someone lending money to someone else. Here are the main things to consider.

The amount. Bonds are sold at an initial price, which is called their *par value*. After that, trading occurs at whatever prices the market will bear.

Issuer. This is the borrower. Check out the firm's or agency's reputation and the bond's quality rating. This is the best way to gauge your chances of being fully repaid with interest.

Yield. This is what you earn, based on the price you pay for the bond.

Maturity. This is when the term of the loan expires. You do not have to stay until the end. You can sell the bonds at any time to anyone willing to take your place as the lender.

Liquidity. It may become necessary to sell the bond early, so check the market to see how easy it will be to sell it.

DEFINING DURATION ▼

The term "duration" is used to describe the time left until a bond matures (the loan ends). This tells you how long until the original investment is returned and you make a gain or a loss.

Investing in Bonds

Different varieties of bonds abound, created to meet all kinds of investing strategies – and all kinds of borrowing needs. Each type offers different advantages and disadvantages.

Choosing UK Government Bonds

Known as gilt-edged securities, these bonds are the primary means of financing government debt. The government pays a fixed rate of interest and promises to repay the debt at an agreed date. Gilts are used by private investors and institutions. They can provide help in the long-term financial planning of a portfolio. Since gilts are issued by the UK Government, investors are usually confident that the initial loan will be repaid. However, gilts may still end up paying a relatively low rate of interest.

Asking the Right Questions

It is important to ask certain questions when you are considering investing some of your money in bonds.

- How much should I lend?
- Is the borrower creditworthy?
- Will I earn enough interest on my loan?
- When and how will I be paid?

Using Gilt Strips

The term "strips" is the acronym for Separately Traded and Registered Interest and Principal Securities. Investing in a gilt strip involves stripping the gilt into its constituent parts: the parts that pay interest and the part that repays the original loan. You can therefore buy gilt strips that either pay a regular flow of interest or repay one lump sum. If you buy bonds at below face value, it is possible to profit from them in the long run. For example, you could buy them at £95 with the promise that they will be redeemed at £100 in a few years. However, make sure you understand the risks involved.

Investing in Convertible Bonds

Some corporate bonds are convertible, meaning they can be exchanged at a specified time for a specific number of shares held by the company that issued the bond. You earn income and can still benefit as an owner if the share price rises. Convertible bonds are usually less volatile in price swings than ordinary shares from the same company, possibly because investors have the added benefit of earning regular income and are therefore less inclined to sell. Generally they also have priority for repayment over common shareholders in cases where the company goes bankrupt.

BUYING PIBS

Permanent Interest Bearing Shares, which are also known as "PIBS", are called shares but act very like bonds. They are issued by major building societies and offer investors a set income. Their capital value moves in response to interest rates. Unlike most gilts, PIBS are not redeemable, so it might be harder to find a buyer. Also, like other investments that carry both interest and capital risks, you should check the creditworthiness of the building society and the terms of the investment first.

17 It is also possible to buy bonds from foreign governments, but check the risks carefully first.

OPTING FOR CORPORATE BONDS

In order to finance major projects, corporations often issue bonds rather than selling shares. The advantage of a corporate bond is that it will often pay a higher rate of interest than that of a government bond. The reason for this is that there is a higher risk that the company will not pay you back. Experts recommend that investors consider the following factors when planning a corporate bond investment:

- The financial quality of the company.
- The company's current profitability.
- The company's long-term financial outlook and stability.

16 Most bonds are free of capital gains tax. However, the Inland Revenue may charge tax if they feel a loophole has been overused.

PUTTING MONEY INTO BOND FUNDS

Bond investments can be a valuable addition to your overall portfolio. However, deciding which bond to buy can be bewildering. You need to consider your needs as an investor and the details of the bond itself. Rather than pick individual bonds, you can invest in a bond fund instead. Just like equity funds, these are managed by professionals who make the decisions about which bonds to buy. If you are considering a bond fund, you should examine its aims and whether it buys relatively risky or safe bonds. The major advantage of a bond fund is that it relieves you from making too many decisions. One of the disadvantages is that the manager takes part of the money as its fee, which reduces the profit you would have made. Nonetheless, it can help spread your risk over more bonds than would be possible if you were investing alone.

OWNING BUSINESSES: BUYING SHARES

Many companies are owned by people like you. To go public, a company divides its ownership into shares and sells them to the public. If you own its shares, you share in the success if it does well, and in the failure if it does not. In short, most people buy shares to let their fortunes ride with the fortunes of the company.

1. DECIDING TO GO PUBLIC

The owners of a small private company need to raise money to stay competitive. They could continue to borrow, but the best way to raise enough money to meet their goals is to ask many people to invest in the company's future. The owners hire an investment banker to take the company public. The banker looks at the company's assets, debts, and profit potential, then calculates how many shares to offer and at what opening price. It is a balancing act. There should not be too many shares, which could flood the market, or too few, which would make shares in short supply. The price should also not be so high as to discourage investors or so low as to fall short of the shares' fair value.

2. SELLING THE SHARES TO THE PUBLIC

On opening day, the shares enter the market as an initial public offering (IPO). The once-private owners are now sharing ownership with the public. Since the shares are new, there is no track record to the share performance and it is therefore even more difficult than usual to judge what will happen to the price.

3. BENEFITING FROM RISING PRICES

The company does not directly receive more money just because its share price rises. However, it still benefits from a rising price because ownership in the company becomes more valuable and says the company is succeeding. Also, rising prices let the management borrow more money, using the value of its shares as collateral.

5. SHARING THE PROFITS

A company's managers may reinvest its earnings until they believe they can share some profits with shareholders and still remain fully competitive. Eventually, they may begin paying a dividend (distributing profits) for every share owned. By this time, you may have sold your shares and may no longer be a shareholder, but others will have taken your place as shareholders, and trading will continue to go round as long as the company remains in business.

4. MONITORING PRICE CHANGES

Research professionals analyze the company and distribute reports to their clients. Every day, people who want to become owners negotiate prices with people who want to sell their shares and get out. Over the long term, the share price will reflect how well a company is performing in its business. In the short term, though, the share price is affected mainly by one thing: supply and demand. If a few people want to sell, but a lot of people want to own the shares, the sellers will drive up their asking price to see just how much the buyers are willing to pay. The price will rise as long as there are people willing to pay higher prices to become an owner. The reverse is also true: if shares become hard to sell, the price will fall until it reaches a level where people are willing to buy.

THINKING LIKE AN OWNER

Shareholders can earn profits in two ways:

- Through distributions of a company's profits, called *dividends*.
- From an increase in the price of a company's shares.

UNDERSTANDING SHARES

There are many types of shares. Different types of shares have different investment qualities. Some also have a higher priority if the company goes bankrupt and will receive payment before other classes of shares.

BUYING ORDINARY SHARES

The fundamental form of ownership in a public company is the shares. Owners of ordinary shares bear the primary burden of business risk but also receive the lion's share of any success.

There are many different ways to group shares, depending on who is doing the grouping. Generally, a share is first looked at as either a growth share (shareholders are looking mainly for price appreciation), or an income share (shareholders own it to earn income from its dividends). Shares are commonly referred to using names based on the life cycle of the company.

Speculative shares. These are shares in relatively new companies who have not yet established themselves in their product or service market. They may also be companies in high-risk businesses, such as the internet, biotechnology, and a number of other highly competitive and money-intensive industries.

Growth shares. These are shares in companies that have moved beyond the phase of uncertainty but still have a lot of room to grow. The more and faster they grow, the more share price movement investors can expect to see.

Value shares. These are shares in well-established companies with histories of consistent earnings and growth.

18 Some investors buy shares of well-known companies for the dividends first, and for the price appreciation potential second.

INVESTING IN BLUE CHIP SHARES

This title is reserved for shares of only the most established companies. They have long histories of solid growth and earnings and a strong foothold in their market.

CHOOSING PREFERENCE SHARES

Some companies offer preference shares. These shares pay a fixed dividend, which is paid before other dividends. If a company has only a limited amount of money, preference shareholders have a better chance of getting paid than ordinary shareholders. If a company goes bust, preference shareholders stand further up the pecking order than ordinary shareholders when it comes to getting a share of the company's remaining value.

SPOTTING UNDERVALUED SHARES

A company's share price may be lower than the actual value of the company due to investor perceptions. For example, the company may have had some negative news that has since been overcome, but investors have not yet recognized the change.

THINGS TO KNOW

- Some shares offer both growth and income potential. A strong, well-established company for example, could be in a booming industry with a lot of growth potential, and also pay attractive dividends.
- Utilities have long been called "income shares" because historically they have paid high dividends and their prices have moved in narrow ranges. People like them because it is felt they offer an essential service that everyone will always need. However, their share price can still move dramatically so they remain a risky investment.
- One way of measuring a share's value is to compare the value of all the shares in the company with the annual earnings of the company. The combined share value of the company, known as its *market capitalization*, is usually a multiple of its yearly earnings. The higher the multiple, the higher the hopes of investors for the company's future earnings. The ratio of share price to earnings is called the *PE ratio* or *Price Earnings ratio*.

GROUPING BY SIZE

Companies are generally grouped into one of four main categories based on their overall market value (the price of the share multiplied by the number of shares in the market).

FTSE 100. The 100 most valuable companies quoted on the London Stock Exchange.

FTSE 250. The next 250 most valuable companies quoted on the Stock Exchange.

FTSE Small Cap. These are the smaller companies quoted on the Stock Exchange.

FTSE Fledglings. These are the smallest companies – many have just started trading.

USING INVESTMENT FUNDS

If you lack the time, interest, or ability to invest on your own, you can join millions of others who give their money to one of thousands of professional money managers who run investment funds. Each fund pools all of its clients' money and invests it according to the general goals and strategies of the fund. By joining forces with many other hard workers who do not want to manage their own money, you gain power to do more than you can do alone.

CREATING LEVERAGE

Investment funds let you use your money as though you were a large investor. The combined resources of many small investors give you enough money to purchase more shares and more securities. Buying in large quantities can also lead to better prices and reduced commissions. Most of all, combining forces with other investors gives you the ability to pay for the services of professional money management.

19 There are savings schemes for as little as £25 a month or a lump sum of £250.

1. BUYING INTO A FUND

You find a fund with a strategy in line with your own. You buy some shares or units in that fund.

2. PRICING THE SHARE

The Net Asset Value (NAV) is calculated by taking the total value of all the fund's assets after all its liabilities have been deducted, then dividing it by the total number of shares or units issued.

3. REASSESSING PRICE

After the markets close every day, the new value of the assets of the fund is calculated and a new NAV is posted for investors to see.

FINDING YOUR FUND

Every fund lists a fund objective that corresponds to one of the three main uses of money: protection, income, or growth (or a combination). This helps you find the right fund for your needs and helps each fund's managers make decisions based on what their clients (like you) expect of them. Different funds may use different strategies to try to achieve their objectives. Marketing brochures will give you a sense of these strategies. Some managers make decisions strictly from mathematical models. Others study a company's business in detail.

THINGS TO KNOW

- Many funds are required to invest only the majority of the money in assets central to the fund's objective. The remaining part may be used to push for higher returns or limit risks using options, futures, foreign securities, currencies, and other sophisticated investments.
- Although an investment trust operates like a fund, it is actually a company and is quoted on the stock exchange. An investment trust invests its shareholders' money in the shares of other companies. They can be traded throughout the day and a price for the sale or purchase of the fund's shares should always be available.

4. SHARING THE COSTS

You share the costs of the fund with all the other investors, such as the managers' salaries, operating expenses, legal and accounting costs, and promotions, based on your percentage of ownership in the fund.

5. SHARING ANY PROFITS

Your shares or units entitle you to a portion of any profits, which can come in three ways:

- Income earned as dividends – even if the fund invests in bonds that earn interest, your payment is still a dividend.
- Capital gains distributed once a year, even though these gains occur any time the manager sells securities from the fund at a profit.
- If you sell shares or units at a higher price (NAV) than you paid, you will earn a profit. If you sell at a lower price, you will take a loss.

PROVIDING FOR RETIREMENT

Although people talk about investing money in a pension, to a large extent it is the annuity that pays them the money back. Over your working life you can contribute to a pension fund. When you retire, you have to use most of it to buy an annuity. The annuity pays you an income for the rest of your life. The more you have in the pension pot, the better the annuity income you will receive.

WEALTH ACCUMULATION PHASE

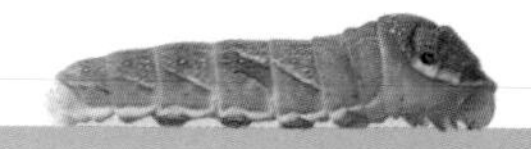

BEGINNING TO INVEST →
You can make a one-time, lump sum payment that puts all your money to work for you immediately or periodic payments that let you add money when you can.

CREATING A MIX →
Often you can invest for growth in share, bond, or cash equivalent products available through the company. You can create a conservative, moderate, or aggressive strategy.

USING TAX BREAKS →
You get tax relief on money paid into a pension – a top-up from the Government at the highest rate of tax you pay.

TRANSFERRING MONEY TAX-FREE

You can move money among the various investment options without incurring taxes on earnings. Removing this obstacle makes it easier to adjust strategies to meet changing needs.

TYING UP YOUR MONEY

Putting money into a pension to buy an annuity has many advantages: it removes the money from temptation and benefits from tax breaks. However, one of the major drawbacks is that it is very difficult to withdraw your money. For that reason you should invest only money that you will not need until you retire.

20 Fees may be deducted every year to cover the pension fund's costs.

21 You may have an option to add a death benefit in case you die during the wealth accumulation phase.

PROVIDING TIME FOR LEISURE
A good annuity can provide you with the time and peace of mind to enable you to stop and smell the flowers.

INCOME MANAGEMENT PHASE

APPROACHING RETIREMENT

For most people this is the crossover point at which you stop contributing to your pension and start benefiting from it. However, you can continue to work and still receive your personal pension benefits. The rules depend on your age and not whether you are working. The two main payment options are shown to the right. Remember that the later you leave it to start saving for your retirement, the more you need to invest to earn a decent pension. So it pays to start investing early.

BUYING AN ANNUITY

You can choose to lock into a guaranteed income plan, in other words an annuity. Most annuities provide a fixed income for the rest of your life. The level of income depends on how old you are and how much you have invested in the annuity.

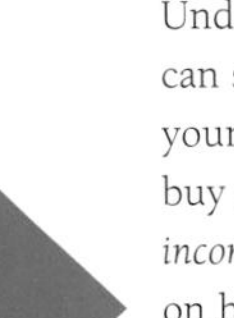

WITHDRAWING AN INCOME

Under certain circumstances you can start to withdraw money from your pension pot without having to buy an annuity. This is called *income drawdown*. There are limits on how much you can take and how old you have to be to gain access to the money.

Exploring Financial Risk

More than anything else, the fear of risk can turn good investment decisions into bad ones, and even stop people from investing entirely. What is risky for one person may not be risky for someone else. It all depends on one's goals and time frame.

Understanding Risk

When you invest, it is important to take the appropriate risk in the context of reaching your goal. If your goal is modest, you can take modest risks. If, however, your goal is challenging, you may face greater risk in getting there, but you may also find ways to reduce the risks and make them more acceptable.

Encountering Financial Risk

The moment you have money – even a pay cheque – you face risk. For example, you could cash the cheque and lose the money. You could put it in a savings account and never earn enough to support yourself in retirement. Even if you do nothing except cash the cheque and store it under your bed, it will be eaten away by inflation. So you should understand that, even by not investing, you are taking risks.

Weighing Risk and Finding the Balance

Every time you have money you have to weigh risks, find the balance, and make your choices. For example, you may need to decide whether to buy now, wait for a sale, or save your money. You may also need to decide whether to carry a little cash around with you, or risk carrying a larger amount.

To find the proper balance in investing, you have to weigh the risks of an investment against the risk of not reaching your goal. Without a goal, you can assess risk by your emotions only.

COMPARING RISK PERSPECTIVES

The common perspective: the greater the risk, the greater the potential for reward. Another perspective: you can easily increase risk without adding potential for reward. So why do it unless you must in order to reach your goal?

The common perspective: certain types of investments are inherently riskier than others. Another perspective: risk depends on how you use the investment. For example, savings accounts are considered to be risk-free, but if you are trying to pay for college tuition, the interest from a savings account will probably leave you short. That is a very big risk.

22 Find out the worst case scenario and ask yourself if you are willing to take that risk.

CONTROLLING RISK

Just because you invest money somewhere – in other words, you let someone else use it – does not mean you have lost control. In fact, the financial world is designed specifically to help people control their risks while letting go of their money. It is a heavily regulated world, where new strategies are constantly being created in the hope of lowering risk without harming the potential for profit. As a beginner, you will use a limited number of strategies to regulate how fast and far to go in reaching your goals. When you become more advanced, however, you can combine different kinds of strategies and even different kinds of investments in attempts to control your risks.

BENEFITING BY TAKING RISKS

Risk is an essential element in investing that you can use to your advantage. For example, it is commonly accepted that yields are higher for bonds that carry a higher risk. However, many of those bonds with higher risk are not risky enough to create problems for most investors. Many therefore accept the higher risk in return for the higher interest they can earn.

23 Asking what the risks are may not be as useful as asking what are the chances of success and failure.

DEALING WITH SHORTFALLS

Shortfall risk is the risk of not reaching (falling short of) your goal. Make no mistake: this is your biggest investment risk – never lose sight of it. Here is an example of how shortfall risk works when you make investment decisions.

DECIDING HOW YOU WILL GET THERE

If you can keep emotions in check, you can look at your goal, where you are now, and how much time you have. Then you can review the types of investments that have at least the potential to bring you to your goal in the time you have available. You need to draw an investment map, which will guide you from where you are to where you want to be. There will be fast, risky roads and smaller, less risky routes.

There is no guarantee that the future will repeat the past, but here is what would have happened to a £100 investment between 1945 and 1999 in the average performance of three investment categories:

- If you had invested your £100 in a bank savings account, by 1999 your investment would have been worth £3,717.
- If you had invested the money in gilt-edged bonds, your investment would have been worth £3,129.
- If you had invested £100 in shares, by 1999 your investment would have been worth £83,284.

(Source: Barclays investment study)

24 Visualizing the future you want will help you achieve your goal.

THIS IS WHERE YOU HOPE TO BE:

£83,284

OTHER FORMS OF INVESTMENT

OVERLOOKING SHORTFALLS

Many financial advisers and finance publications do not mention shortfall risk. One reason why it may be overlooked so often is that the financial industry is still learning to focus more on you than on investment products.

MINIMIZING THE EFFECTS OF A SHORTFALL

As the illustration shows, only an investment in large company shares would have allowed you to reach your goal on time.

The strategies some people might consider to be more conservative – bond investments, for example – would have left you falling far short of your goal. The further you fall short, the more you have to do to finance the difference. To fill the gap and reach your goal without taking the appropriate level of risk, you would need to:

- Invest more money each year, so you would have more money earning and compounding for you.
- Finance the shortfall through other means. If your goal is to fund college tuition, for example, you might decide to take cash from the equity in your home, take another form of loan, or get other forms of financial assistance (for example, grants and scholarships). However, loans cost money in terms of fees and interest and those expenses will reduce the amount of your wealth.

UNDERSTANDING INFLATION

Anyone with any money needs to understand inflation – how it affects you and how to protect yourself from it.

25 The Retail Price Index (RPI) measures the change in the cost of goods and services.

DEFINING INFLATION

The term "inflation" refers to price increases. However, a better word might be disintegration because, like milk that goes sour and fruit that rots, money is a perishable item that is constantly disintegrating, even though it is difficult for most of us to see. Every year, the value of our money disintegrates at a pace equal to the inflation rate, so that every year your money will buy less than it did the year before.

If you do not pay attention to inflation, you will never notice how much of your money disappears from year to year, as if simply turning to dust and blowing away

into nothingne

LOSING MONEY

Say you put aside £100 today to buy a £100 coat next year. If prices inflate by 3% for the year, the coat will cost £103. It would be as though you lost 3% of your money without doing anything.

BEING AWARE OF YOUR EARNINGS

It is important to know how much your money is earning. However, to understand what you will eventually get, it is just as important to know how much your money is losing.

EARNING INTEREST ON YOUR MONEY
You earn a certain amount of interest from an investment. This percentage may be the figure you use to plan your budget for the next year.

LOSING SOME MONEY THROUGH INFLATION
Your money loses some of its buying power every year. In Germany before World War II, inflation was so high that money would lose almost all of its value literally overnight. People actually found the money more valuable as fireplace kindling.

KNOWING WHAT YOU HAVE LEFT AFTER INFLATION
Subtracting the percentage lost to inflation from the percentage your money earned, you are actually left with 3.65%. That, in industry terms, is called the real rate of return *– a very appropriate name.*

EXPLORING CAUSES OF INFLATION

Inflation can be caused by having too much money in circulation (high employment can create too much spending money, or the Government may be printing a lot of money).

Inflation can also be caused by shortages. If there is a shortage of raw materials or of a product itself, producers may pay higher prices and pass them on to consumers.

HANDLING MARKET RISK

Market risk is what keeps some people out of the stock market. It is simply the chance that an investment will lose value after you buy it. What makes market risk particularly intimidating to beginners is that it is unpredictable. Seasoned investors, however, are not so threatened because, while unpredictable, market risk is acceptable, somewhat manageable, and sometimes even desirable – at least temporarily.

UNDERSTANDING WHY PRICES CHANGE

Virtually every investment goes up and down in price – gains and loses value – over time. Prices reflect the public's fears and hopes, affecting supply and demand.

Take a share for example. If there are many buyers and not enough sellers, the price will rise until it is high enough to induce owners of the share to sell. If there are too many sellers, the price will eventually drop low enough to where it induces new investors to buy.

Even a share that is rising steadily may fall in price for at least a day, if there are more investors wanting to sell and take profits than there are new buyers.

ASSESSING VOLATILITY

How often and quickly an investment's price can change is called its *price volatility*. Think of it as a sensitivity to market conditions. For example, if a small event causes a price to rise or fall, then the investment is volatile. If the price stays calm while others move, it is considered stable.

PREPARING FOR A BUMPY RIDE ▼

Investment prices go up and down like a train ride through the mountains. In fact, if you look at a price chart for a share, it is not hard to imagine it as the track of a train, or even of a rollercoaster.

Rising price
This price rise is gradual, but rises are often steep. A low-quality bond can rise and fall in price as quickly and as sharply as a volatile share.

Declining price
Here, the price starts a decline. This time it is gradual, but prices can drop sharply.

Steadying price
For a while, the price levels out and the investors' ride is smooth and steady.

MANAGING RISK

Here is what many experts recommend. None of these are hard-and-fast rules.

Do not buy high and sell low. Although it is not a foolproof guarantee, try to avoid buying when a price is historically high or selling when a price is historically low.

Do not jump on bandwagons. Try not to invest in something because everyone you know has already made a profit and you want to profit too. It may be too late.

Pay attention to time. Avoid volatile securities if you:

- Are close to achieving your goals and will soon be ready to sell.
- May need the money for an emergency. Timing is crucial to managing market risk. The key is to avoid situations where you could be forced to sell when prices are down, and therefore take a loss simply because you had no choice.

Invest for the long term. Generally speaking, those who plan to stay in an investment for at least five years can ignore the daily ups and downs in prices.

THINGS TO KNOW

- You can get a sense of a share's price volatility before investing by taking a look at its *beta*. You can ask your broker for this or search for it in the share profile from an online site. Beta measures a share's volatility compared to the whole market. A beta of 1 means a share is no more or less sensitive to price changes than the overall market. The higher the number is over 1, the more sensitive the share. The lower the number is below 1, the less sensitive the share.
- When the price of an investment is high and then drops, it can create a *buying opportunity*. This means investors think the investment is now cheap enough to make it worth buying – or buying more. It is similar to buying a product on sale for a limited time. However, just because the price has fallen does not mean it is cheap. If the investment is no longer as attractive as it once was, the price may fall even further.

Moving unpredictably
On a train, you can look ahead and see the peaks and valleys. Price changes are not as easy to spot.

26 It is not uncommon for a share price to fluctuate 50% or more during any given year.

UNDERSTANDING INTEREST RATE RISK

Changes in our economy's interest rates affect the value of many investments, particularly bonds and other fixed income securities. Some inexperienced bond investors do not worry about the value of their bonds as long as they earn the interest expected. This is fine for anyone holding a bond until maturity (when the initial investment is repaid in full). For everyone else, however, changes in bond prices are as important as changes in share prices.

RISING RATES, FALLING PRICES

As rates rise, securities that pay interest tend to fall in price. Bonds that are initially sold for £1,000 (par value) may be resold at any time for whatever the investors will pay. If interest rates were to rise, investors would be able to buy newly issued bonds for £1,000 that pay more than your bond. In this scenario, you would have to sell your bond for less than you paid (and take a loss) in order to entice a seller to take it with its lower interest.

ASSESSING HOW INTEREST RATES AFFECT SHARES

When interest rates rise, many investors sell shares and buy bonds or put the money in a bank or building society. This is because when interest rates rise, they increase the amount you make in a deposit account. Since there is little risk attached to deposit accounts, the rise in interest rates makes them more attractive in comparison with the risky stock market.

SOME BONDS ARE CALLABLE

Some bonds have a built-in protection clause for the issuers. The clause says that when interest rates drop, the issuer can *call* the bond, which means the issuer can repay you the original amount you paid and end the loan. This is essentially the right to prepay the loan in full without penalty before the due date. Callability gives bond issuers the ability to refinance at lower rates and lower their operational costs, but it creates a risk for investors. They will have to reinvest the money and earn less interest, or pay more to earn the same interest.

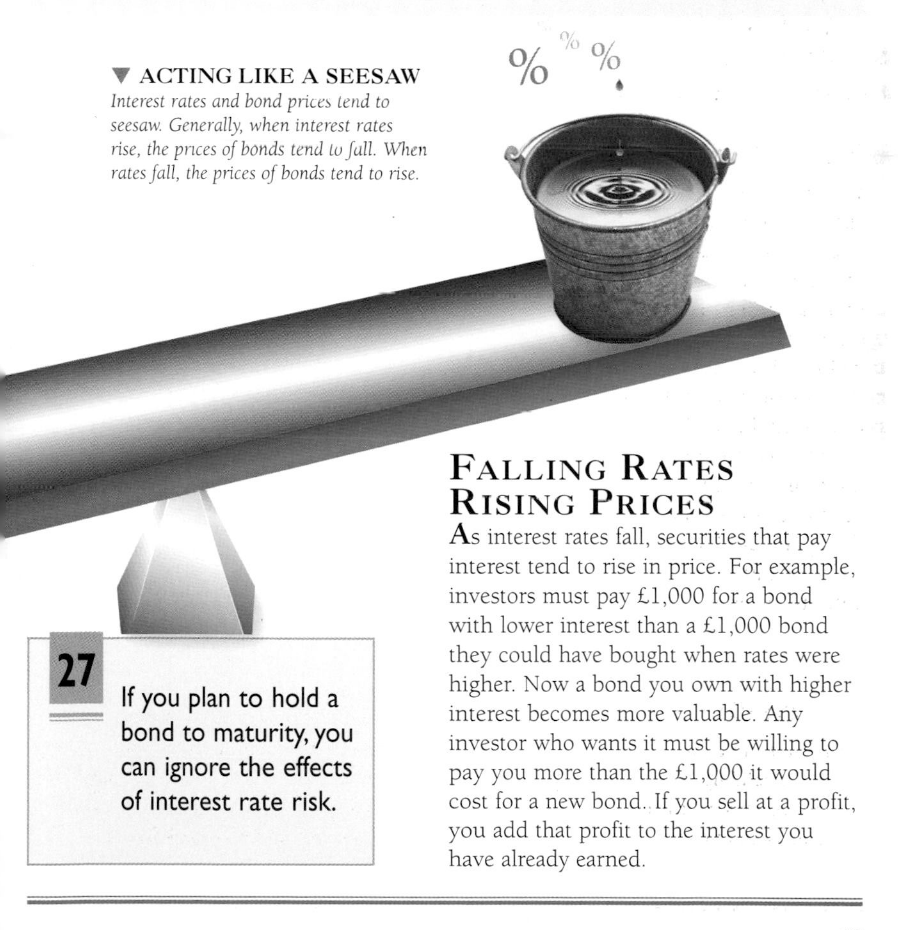

▼ ACTING LIKE A SEESAW
Interest rates and bond prices tend to seesaw. Generally, when interest rates rise, the prices of bonds tend to fall. When rates fall, the prices of bonds tend to rise.

FALLING RATES RISING PRICES

As interest rates fall, securities that pay interest tend to rise in price. For example, investors must pay £1,000 for a bond with lower interest than a £1,000 bond they could have bought when rates were higher. Now a bond you own with higher interest becomes more valuable. Any investor who wants it must be willing to pay you more than the £1,000 it would cost for a new bond. If you sell at a profit, you add that profit to the interest you have already earned.

27

If you plan to hold a bond to maturity, you can ignore the effects of interest rate risk.

ASSESSING CREDIT RISK

The safety of your investment is subject partly to the creditworthiness of the business or government in which you are investing. This is called credit risk. *To assess credit risk, you have to look at your investment in the same way a lender would look at making a loan to you.*

INVESTING IN SHARES

By investing in a company, you are showing faith in its potential success. As a result, you expect its share price to rise. Part of a company's success may come from its ability to borrow money at good rates when needed. Lenders assess a company's credit the same way they assess yours. In other words, they question the company's:

- Cash, income, and debt to see if it has the financial strength to repay what it borrows.
- History of repayment to see how well it has repaid other loans.

A company's credit rating is not always readily available to the average investor, but an adviser can help you assess financial strength by looking at the company's annual report.

CHOOSING BONDS

By investing in bonds, you are showing faith in the promises of interest and repayment made to you by the issuer. The safety of your bond investment has a lot to do with the creditworthiness of the company or government standing behind the bond. To assess risk, the bond market relies on independent ratings agencies that continually monitor the financial strength and credit histories of bond issuers. Typically, a bond issuer with:

- Strong credit can borrow money at low rates and still attract investors.
- Poor credit has to offer higher interest rates to attract investors.

Just because something is a credit risk does not mean it is not worth the investment.

USING RATINGS SERVICES

The financial world relies heavily on the credit reports issued by the two largest independent ratings services: Moody's and Standard & Poor's. They provide standardized, internationally recognized systems to rate the strength of many bonds issued by corporations and governments. A bond's rating is continually monitored and revised, keeping the investment world informed about the issuer's ongoing level of creditworthiness. Many marketing brochures pitching fixed income investment funds refer to these ratings. The table below should help you sort out what the ratings mean. You will also find more details on creditworthiness in any fixed income investment fund prospectus.

BUYING JUNK BONDS

Just like people with poor credit, the issuers of junk bonds have poor credit and are therefore less likely to repay their debt as promised. This does not automatically translate into a bad investment, however. Many investors are willing to accept the risk in exchange for the higher interest that junk bond issuers are willing to pay to attract the money they need.

EXPLANATION	MOODY'S	STANDARD & POOR'S
Bonds of highest quality with the greatest likelihood of repaying in full with interest.	Aaa	AAA
Very strong credit. There is not much difference from the highest rating.	Aa	AA
Still reliable, but may be susceptible to problems in the future.	A	A
Medium-grade. Normally, these are adequate, but have the capacity to weaken in adverse economic conditions.	Baa	BBB
This is the cutoff point for bonds considered to be "investment grade".		
Bonds with few desirable credit characteristics. Moody's considers them to have speculative aspects.	Ba	BB
Primarily speculative bonds. They carry considerable uncertainty and risk in adverse conditions.	B	B
Highly speculative with poor credit. The lower the rating, the more likely to default.	Caa Ca	CCC CC, C, C1
Lowest rating, usually in default. Little likelihood of being repaid.	C	D

FINDING WAYS TO MANAGE RISK

Since risks cannot be avoided, a major part of any strategy is to manage the risks involved. Here are some effective strategies for both beginners and advanced investors.

WORKING WITH TIME

Everything changes over time. This makes timing a critical part of every decision you make about what to do with your money. Whether you buy or sell, lend or borrow, time is a double-edged sword to be used thoughtfully. Time can raise or lower your potential risks and rewards, depending on how you manage it.

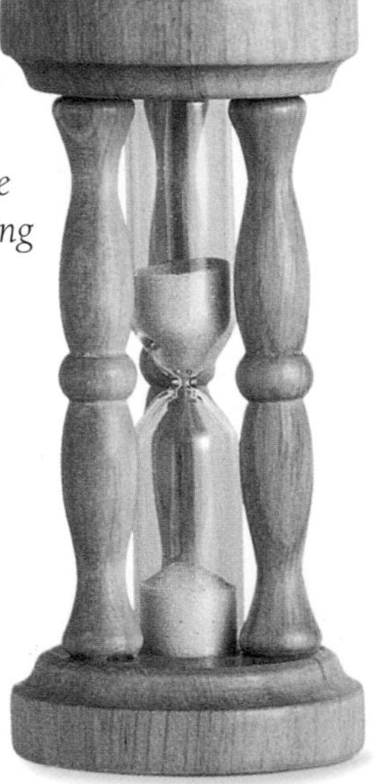

DEFINING GOALS AND ASSESSING TIME

The risks of time are put into perspective when you have a goal. Without a goal, how can you know what is too long or what is not long enough? When you know your goals and how much time you have, your perspective on potential problems changes.

WATCHING HOW TIME AFFECTS BONDS

In the world of bonds, more time typically means more risk.

Short-term use. If you let go of your money only for short stretches, you reduce the amount of time for something to go wrong. However, the less time your money has to work hard, the less money you are likely to earn. With less risk comes less earning potential.

Long-term use. If you let go of your money for long stretches, you lose some control and subject yourself to more risks. However, you can earn more because time gives your money more opportunities to grow.

ADJUSTING YOUR PACE TO SUIT YOUR GOALS

If you have far to go in a short time, you will have to go faster. If you have a long time, you can go more slowly. As everyone knows, speeding is usually riskier than going slowly – but not always. Just as slow drivers may never reach their destinations on time, overprotective investors may never reach their goals on time. Look at each potential investment within the context of your goals. Then weigh the likelihood that good things might happen (the potential reward) versus the likelihood that bad things might happen (the risk) within the time you have left.

Shares tend to do better than most other types of investments over the long term.

KNOWING HOW TIME AFFECTS SHARES

Since shares, as a group, carry the most market risk and issues of volatility, it might seem that a long-term investment in shares would be at greater risk than a short-term investment. But historically, time has tended to make shares, as a group, one of the lowest-risk investments.

Short-term use. If you have short-term goals, short-term rises and drops can look uncomfortably volatile to you. After all, you run the risk of having to sell your shares and get your money out during a short-term dip in price.

Long-term use. If you have a long-term goal, you can take a broader, calmer, more studied view of the circumstances. You can afford to ride out a short-term rollercoaster ride and feel more secure that if shares continue to repeat their history, the dips will merely seem part of an overall trend that has gone up.

FINE-TUNING CONTROL

Each of these elements can be managed along a spectrum of control, from more control to less, from less trust to greater trust in others.

MANAGING INVESTMENTS

Doing it yourself. Keeping full control of your investments – creating your plan, finding opportunities, making investment decisions, and so forth – is a way of running your investing business on your own. But do-it-yourself investing is not like building a deck or fixing a water heater. It requires frequent and ongoing maintenance, review, study, and decision making. Be sure you have the time, energy, resources, understanding, and confidence to do it yourself. Otherwise, like any other business, delegate some responsibilities to people who are better at certain tasks than you are. However, you are the boss and need to stay involved.

Getting help. You can get help from books, discount brokers, full-service brokers, investment funds, on-line, or even hire your own professional money manager. You should research all your options carefully.

DOING IT YOURSELF ▼

Investing can be a do-it-yourself endeavour, just like anything else.

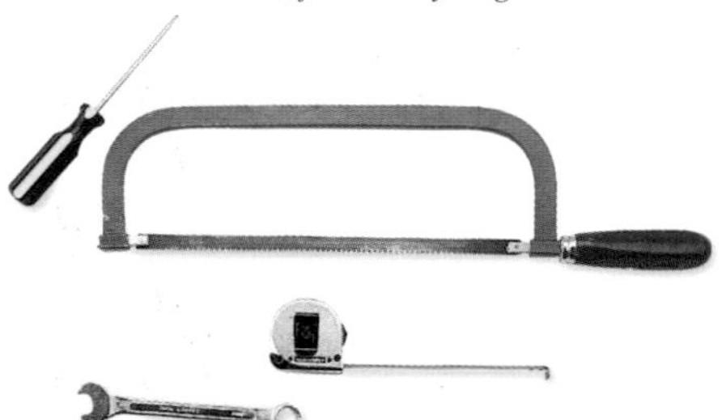

MAKING CHOICES

The type of investment you select is another way to control your money.

Owning. If you choose to become an owner in a company (by buying shares), then you are giving up control over that money indefinitely. This means you could take back your money (sell) that same day or many years later. Most importantly, you are letting your money be used any way the company's management wants to use it. So you have to have faith in the business and trust the way the management will run it. Depending upon your percentage of ownership in the company, you may have very little control, if any, over whether or not the company will do well.

Lending. If you choose to lend money (buy bonds), then your money will be unavailable for any other use during the time restrictions. Most bonds have no restrictions. You may sell them whenever you wish. Keep in mind, though, that bond prices fluctuate just as share prices do, even if with less frequency and degree. So you could decide to sell a bond at a time when the price is less than you paid, and take a loss. You can buy bonds in the hope of trading with them and selling at a profit, in which case the price fluctuations will be important to you.

USING TIME

Time plays a crucial and constant role in controlling investments.

Investing for the short term. If you cannot trust that your money will be used with respect for your needs, or if you expect to need your money soon, then you can invest in a savings account or a money market fund where the money is invested for very short periods (often overnight). These short-term investments do not leave much time for anything to go wrong, and the people using your money take virtually no chances with it. In exchange for the protection, you earn only a little money.

Opting for intermediate term. If you want to earn more, you can allow people to use your money for longer periods (defined by the industry typically as between five and fifteen years). In exchange for the longer time, people typically pay more for that privilege. There is also more time for something to go wrong, however, and affect either your ability to get your money or to earn what you expect. However, in most cases, you can sell your investment to someone else, get some or all of your money back, and let another investor take any further risks.

Choosing the long-term option. Generally, you can earn the most if you make investments that allow others to use your money for long periods of time. In the case of bonds, that can be as long as thirty years. (You do not have to stay invested that long. You can sell your investment to someone else and let that person continue with the risks and rewards.) Since your willingness to let your money be used for long periods is usually met with a promise to pay you more for that privilege, the longer the term, the higher the interest tends to be. You are being compensated (even induced) to take the risks.

USING MONEY

Whether you own a company or lend money, the way in which your money will be used is critical to its safety. Who is getting your money and how they plan to use it are both important considerations.

Deciding on acceptability. If you invest in the shares of a very young, aggressive company, for example, you are accepting the fact that your money may be used for very aggressive, high-risk purposes, or that the company may not stay competitive and may even go out of business. Such companies may offer the promise of much larger rewards, if the gamble pays off and they develop new markets. However, if the venture is not a success, you can lose all your money. If you invest in a solid entity and/or in a solid use of the money, the reverse is more true. In short, you decide which people and which uses are acceptable or unacceptable to you.

Trusting the borrower. You have to trust the creditworthiness of the borrower. You also have to assess the soundness of how your money will be used by the borrower.

▲ CREATING OPPORTUNITIES

Time can be a double-edged sword, opening more opportunities for positive as well as negative events to occur.

DIVERSIFYING YOUR PORTFOLIO

How do you know which investments are the right ones? Spreading your money among a variety of investments that react differently to different events is a simple strategy you can use to manage risk.

SPREAD RISK IN SHARES BY:

USING GROWTH AND PRICE POTENTIAL

- As a well-known quantity, the bigger, well-established companies may not grow dramatically but they may offer the most price stability.
- Mid-sized, established companies may have more room to grow but may also offer less price stability than the big companies.
- Small and start-up companies may offer the most growth potential but are also probably the most likely to be sensitive to price swings.

SPREAD RISK IN BONDS BY:

CHOOSING THE MOST SUITABLE TYPE OF BOND

To whom do you want to lend your money? The kind of issuer – corporation or government body – can affect the level of investment safety and whether or not income is taxable. Bonds can be:

- Gilts (otherwise known as gilt-edged securities). These are bonds issued by the Government and are considered to be at low risk of default. However, gilt prices can still fluctuate, so if you do not hold on until maturity they can be risky.
- Corporate bonds (issued by companies). The risk of these bonds depends on which company issued them.

OPTING FOR ▶ SHARES OR BONDS
Shares and bonds are different animals and should not be confused with each other.

DECIDING HOW TO EARN MONEY

- Some shares pay out some profits as dividends, offering regular income.
- Growth shares reinvest profits to try to keep growing. This helps the share price to grow, but means you will not earn money until you sell.
- Some shares offer both growth and income opportunities.

INVESTING GLOBALLY

You can capture profits in growing economies and minimize losses in unhealthy market climates by investing money globally in:

- Stable, industrialized countries.
- Less predictable, emerging growth countries.

SELECTING INDUSTRIES

What type of industry interests you? There are many industries. Some do better than others in different economic climates.

JUDGING QUALITY

A bond's credit rating reflects the balance between safety and how much interest it pays. You can buy:

- High-quality bonds, which usually offer a higher level of safety but lower interest.
- Lower-quality bonds, which usually offer a lower level of safety but higher interest.
- Junk bonds, which usually offer the lowest level of safety but the highest interest rate.

TIMING YOUR LOANS

You can mix the certainty of short-term loans with the higher income of longer-term loans. You can choose:

- Long-term bonds, which usually offer higher interest rates but the most volatility in terms of price.
- Intermediate bonds, which usually offer mid-range interest rates and mid-range price volatility.
- Short-term bonds, which usually offer the lowest interest rates but the most stability in terms of price.

UNDERSTANDING POUND COST AVERAGING

When is it a good time to invest? What is a good price? You can manage the market risk with an easy strategy called pound cost averaging.

HELPING NOVICES AND SMALL INVESTORS

This most basic of strategies is good for beginners who are nervous about investing, or at least uncomfortable with using their money in a way that they do not fully understand. It is also good for people who can afford to invest only small amounts of money at a time.

▼ GETTING INTO ACTION

Below is an example of pound cost averaging in action. For simplicity, this example excludes all commissions and other costs. All you do is give your broker £500 to invest in the same share each month, no matter what the price.

DAY 1

The share price is £5. You invest £500. That buys 100 shares.

DAY 31 (MONTH 2)

The share price is now £16.67. You invest £500. That buys 30 shares. Total shares: 130. Your average price per share = £7.69.

DAY 61 (MONTH 3)

The share price is £8. You invest £500. That buys 62 shares. Total shares: 192. Your average price per share = £7.81.

REMOVING THE GUESSWORK

Pound cost averaging offers you choices. You can invest:

- In shares, bonds, or investment funds.
- On a regular schedule automatically.
- Any amount of money you want for each investment.

ACCUMULATING SHARES IN STAGES

The point is to accumulate a lot of shares over time without using a lot of money each time. Since you are not investing all at once, you do not need to have much money to get started. You may even be able to stick to the plan by transferring money directly from your bank account each month.

30 For many, the purpose of pound cost averaging is simply to become an investor, even if they have only a little to invest.

USING A THREE-PART PLAN

There are three parts to pound cost averaging:
The investment. You select the type of fund in which to invest.
The timing. You select a regularly scheduled date that coincides with your pay cheque (or another logical time).
The amount. You select the amount you feel you can afford to invest at each interval (for example, an amount you will not miss and that you might otherwise have spent on impulsive purchases).

As the example below shows, you could decide to invest £500 in a fund on the first day of each month. Then you pick a date to make the first investment – and the process begins.

DAY 91 (MONTH 4)

The share price is up to £9. You invest £500. That buys 55 shares. Total shares: 247. Your average price per share = £8.10.

DAY 121 (MONTH 5)

The share price is £6. You invest £500. That buys 83 shares. Total shares: 330. Your average price per share = £7.58.

STICKING TO THE PLAN

Once you begin, you should stick with the plan – no matter what happens to the price. You will find that sometimes your money will buy more shares, while at other times it will buy fewer shares.

KNOWING YOUR PSYCHOLOGY

If you are buying as the price goes down, will you be the kind of investor who wonders whether you are throwing good money after bad on a poor choice? Or will you trust your initial decision to buy those shares, that the price will rise eventually, and consider yourself lucky to have a chance to buy more shares at bargain prices?

REBALANCING ASSETS

Over time, some of your investments may prove to be stronger performers than others. That tips the balance of your original mix. On a regular basis, it makes sense to review your goals and strategies to see whether you may have to adjust some investments to return the mix to a balance that works best for you.

UNDERSTANDING REBALANCING

Investments change in value all the time and, as they do, they become either a larger or smaller percentage of your overall investment portfolio. To counteract these natural, ongoing shifts in percentages, investors periodically *rebalance* their investment portfolios to the originally intended mix. This enables investors to keep their strategy on course to meet their goals.

DECIDING HOW TO REBALANCE

To rebalance, you sell some investments that rose in value and, with that money, buy more of the investments that did not keep pace. There are two ways to rebalance.

Static rebalancing. This is the strict approach. You set percentages, then regularly return each asset group to that original percentage regardless of market conditions or your outlook for the market.

Tactical rebalancing. This approach gives you flexibility to shift your target percentages slightly to factor in market conditions and your own outlook. Rather than stick to strict targets, you can shift percentages within an acceptable range.

REBALANCING IN ACTION

You simply move some money from the asset group that is above its original percentage into the asset group that is below its original percentage, as the chart below illustrates.

STARTING MIX:	AFTER A YEAR:	TO REBALANCE:
50% in shares	65% in shares	sell surplus 15% of share funds
30% bond funds	25% bond funds	put one-third into bond funds
20% cash equivalents	10% cash equivalents	put two-thirds into cash equivalents

BENEFITING FROM REBALANCING

The most important reason to rebalance a portfolio is to keep on track with your goals. However, there are also other benefits.

Risk control. It keeps you from taking more risk than you intended. Say, for example, you started with 50% of your money in shares, and it grew to 75% of your portfolio. That might be a riskier portfolio than the one you had in mind, especially if your funds have a history of higher-than-average market risk.

Growth potential. On the other hand, say you started with 50% in share funds, and it dropped in value to 40% of your portfolio. Now you would have less of your money allocated for growth potential than you first intended. You might sell some of your bond funds and invest the proceeds in the shares to have 50% of your assets there again. However, the strategy can also force you to buy shares that are falling in price, so do not follow rules slavishly.

Locking in profits. "Buy low, sell high" is one of the cornerstones of successful investing. Therefore some strategies, like rebalancing, force you to sell investments that have gone up in value and buy more of those that have dropped in value. Why? It helps lock in profits from investments that have risen instead of tempting you to try to squeeze out a little more profit by holding on to your investments longer.

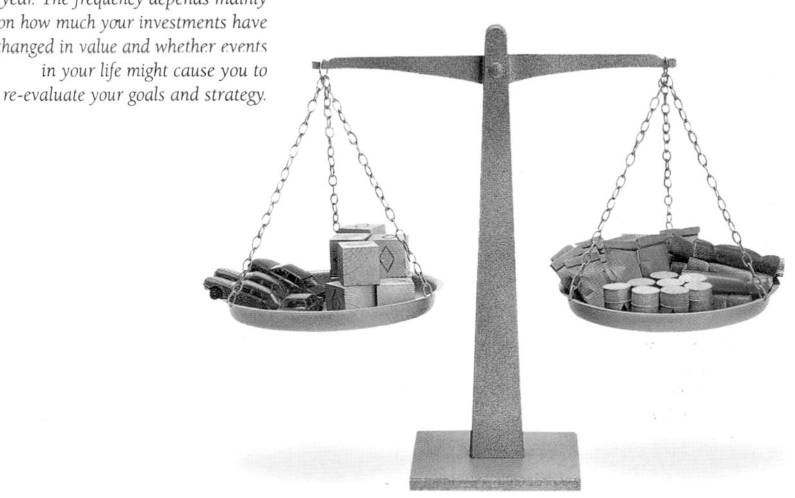

REBALANCING ON A REGULAR BASIS ▼

Many experts recommend rebalancing at regular intervals, at least once a year. The frequency depends mainly on how much your investments have changed in value and whether events in your life might cause you to re-evaluate your goals and strategy.

UNDERSTANDING PERFORMANCE

Investing is all about performance – how much money you make. There are a number of ways to assess how well your investments are doing in helping you reach your goals.

ASSESSING WHAT YOU EARN

The most obvious way to assess performance is by looking at how much your investments are earning.

KNOWING YOUR TAX LIABILITIES

Investments can produce two different types of earnings:

Ordinary income. Bonds pay interest and some shares pay dividends. These kinds of earnings are classed as ordinary income. That is important for tax reasons because as ordinary income they will be taxed at your usual tax band rate.

Capital gains. If you sell at a higher price than you paid, your profit minus any commissions will be classed as a capital gain. Under current tax rules, capital gains under a certain amount each year are exempt from tax. Ask your tax adviser for details.

Pumping Premiums

Generally, if you buy a bond at an initial price of £1,000 each, you will be repaid £1,000 at maturity (the end of the loan). Sometimes, to give their fund the appearance of high performance, or to give shareholders a temporary high return, investment fund managers will pay a premium (over £1,000) for bonds with above-average interest. If the fund still holds that bond when it matures, the fund – and you – will take a loss. Say that you are the only shareholder in a fund with only one bond. It cost £1,000 when issued and pays 5% (£50) a year, but when interest rates elsewhere drop to 4.5%, your fund buys it for £1,100. A year from now, the bond matures and the fund is paid only £1,000. In short, it lost £100, wiping out the £50 in interest you earned for the year, leaving you with an actual loss of £50.

Defining Gains

When your investment goes up in value but you do not sell it, you have *unrealized gains*. The common term for that is *paper profits*, because your profit is only on your statement. Only when you sell at a profit do you make the gain a reality, called a *realized gain* by the industry.

Things to Know

- Many investors simply look at articles or advertisements for investment funds with the highest returns, then invest in those. A fund that performs well today, though, might not perform well tomorrow. After all, investing means buying something for its future performance – not yesterday's performance. Economic climates change, investment managers leave, investments fall out of favour, companies lose business, and so on – there are many factors that have the potential to change the performance of a fund.
- The axiom "buy low, sell high" should serve as a reminder that if you buy high, there may be more chance that you will eventually be selling lower.
- Performance is not the only thing that matters. Running costs also count. Look at the small print and see how much managers are charging to run the fund. If their fee is higher than that of their competitors, ask why, and include the fact in your thinking when making a decision about whether or not to invest. The extra charge may be worthwhile, but you need to check it against performance figures as a whole.
- Performance numbers listed in advertisements may not take into account the fees you pay for investing in a fund. A fund with an 8% return, for example, may have lower costs than a fund with an 8.5% return, leaving you with more money in your pocket.

CALCULATING COSTS

Smart investing means understanding that expenses lower performance. In other words, every penny you pay as a sales charge or other fee will directly reduce your profit. So it makes sense to look at what an investment will actually cost you, not just at how much it might earn.

ASSESSING THE COSTS OF SHARES AND BONDS

There are two main fees for buying and selling shares and bonds. One is obvious; the other is not so obvious.

Commission. Typically, every time you buy or sell a share or bond, you pay a commission to your broker. That is easy to see because the amount appears on the order confirmation you receive. With the growth of on-line trading, brokers are competing for business by aggressively lowering commissions.

The spread. You may think that if you pay a price for a share, the seller will receive that price as the sales price. That is not how it works. There is something called the *spread*. It is the middleman's profit – the difference between the price a buyer pays and the price the seller receives. The chart below shows how it works.

CALCULATING YOUR PROFIT

MID PRICE	THE ASK	THE SPREAD	THE BID	COMMISSION
£20	£20	50P	£19.50	49P
You bought one share at £18, and now that the price is £20, you want to sell. It looks like a £2 gain.	The "ask" is the price all buyers pay. However, you are selling, not buying, so this price is not yours.	This is the profit for the *specialist* who is facilitating trades in that share. In this case, the spread is 50p a share.	This is the price all sellers receive. Since you are a seller, you receive £19.50.	You pay a broker a commission of 20p to sell your share. Now you receive £19.30. However, you also paid a 20p commission to buy it, plus stamp duty of 9p, so you are actually down to £19.01.

31 A fund with a 7.5% return and 0.5% in fees will give you a greater net profit than a fund with an 8% return and 1.5% in fees.

PAYING STAMP DUTY

Stamp duty is a tax levied by the Government on all share purchases, but not sales. This means that, whenever you buy shares, you will have to pay an additional 0.5% of the purchase price for stamp duty.

ASSESSING COSTS OF TRACKER FUNDS

The management fee – the fund manager's salary – is a major expense of an investment fund. Tracker funds are unmanaged, because trading occurs based on a computer model that tracks an index, not on a manager's subjective decisions. This makes tracker funds less costly than what are called actively managed funds. That means a tracker fund does not have to perform as well to provide you with the same return on your money.

UNDERSTANDING PORTFOLIO TURNOVER

The portfolio turnover tells you how often securities in the fund are bought and sold ("turned over"). The fund pays a commission to its broker every time a trade is made. This expense reduces the fund's – and your – profit. Turnover is shown as a percentage: the higher the percentage is, the higher the expenses.

KNOWING INVESTMENT FUND COSTS

Investment funds will often charge an initial fee on joining the fund and an annual management fee on top of that. The higher the charges, the better the fund has to perform in order to pay you a profit. Not all funds charge the same and the value of the fund to you will depend on a combination of how well it performs and how much the fund manager charges. Make sure you know all of the charges being made before you put your money into the fund.

EXPLORING THE MARGARINE MARKET

The difference between the buying price and selling price is called the spread. The size of the spread is not constant, it differs from hour to hour and day to day. You will often find that in the early morning, spreads are wider than in the afternoon. Since the spread can be very wide in the morning, the morning market is often called the margarine market.

COMPARING PERFORMANCE

The financial industry has developed a tool for comparing your investment's performance against other similar investments. It is called an index, *which is a measurement of the combined average performance of groups of similar securities.*

USING TRACKING DEVICES

When you hear that the market went up or went down, you are actually hearing about an index, which is a general indicator of market performance. Here are only some of the many indexes and other tracking devices that are in existence today.

The FTSE 100. This is the main index used by most commentators. It tracks the performance of the most valuable 100 companies listed on the London Stock Exchange.

The FTSE 250. Less widely used, this index tracks the performance of the next most valuable 250 shares listed on the London Stock Exchange.

The FTSE 350. This index combines the FTSE 100 and FTSE 250 and gives a much wider picture of what is happening across the main UK stock market.

The FTSE All Share. Contrary to its name, the FTSE All Share index does not include all shares but it does track the performance of the vast majority of them and gives a very broad picture of what is happening across the UK stock market as a whole.

The Dow. The most famous US index is the Dow Jones Industrial Average (DJIA). It is a formula created (and sometimes revised) by the editors of The Wall Street Journal. The Dow Jones index tracks the daily gains and losses of thirty companies from the New York Stock Exchange that the editors consider to be key players in the market and the economy. Whether you believe it to be right or wrong, their theory is this: as these thirty companies go, so goes the market. Today, experts refer to this theory as being based more on sentiment than on an accurate measure of market performance.

Nasdaq Composite. This index measures the performance of the entire Nasdaq exchange – over 5,500 US companies. The further we move into the information age, the more this index may become relevant because the majority of internet and other high-tech companies in the United States are listed on the Nasdaq.

CAC 40. This is the main index that tracks the 40 most valuable shares on the Paris stock market in France.

▲ **ASSESSING PERFORMANCE**
Monitor the performance of your investments and make comparisons with the performance of other investments to judge how well you are doing.

DAX 30. The DAX 30 is the main index that tracks the 30 most valuable shares listed on the Frankfurt stock market in Germany.
Exchange Traded Funds. A relatively new addition to the investment supermarket, these allow you to track an index without buying a traditional tracker fund. Exchange traded funds are quoted on the stock market and you can therefore get a price at any time during market hours. They are cheaper to invest in than most funds and, since you can buy and sell so quickly, they allow you to respond to market changes more effectively than some traditional tracking investments.

LEARNING HOW TO MAKE COMPARISONS

How do you compare the performance of different kinds of investments, such as a bond, an investment fund, and a share? You can look at a performance figure called the *annual total return*. To assess an investment's annual total return, you do the following:

- Add an investment's total amount of interest or dividends earned for the year to the change in price since the beginning of the year.
- Then subtract the annual expenses (which applies to investment funds) including commissions (which can apply to bonds, shares, and investment funds).

All investment funds have an easy-to-read section in the prospectus that tells you the annual returns for that fund. Using that section, you do not have to do any calculations yourself to compare a variety of different investment funds. You can simply compare the average annual total returns for each fund.

32 Use an index to take a quick reading of how the kind of investment you own is doing.

STUDYING THE EFFECTS OF TAXES

Taxes are a significant factor in investing performance because they go right to the bottom line and reduce the amount of earnings you get to keep. They are often overlooked by investors, particularly when considering whether to sell a security and take a profit. Here are the main taxes on investments.

PAYING TAX ON ORDINARY INCOME

Most investment income is liable for tax in the same way as a salary. Therefore in most cases the higher your tax bracket, the more you will have to pay out in taxes from your investment earnings.

THINGS TO KNOW

- Many people do not realize that it is common for a company or an investment fund to declare a dividend on a certain date and then pay you a few weeks later. You are required to report dividends as income on your tax returns, and for tax purposes the date to use is the date when the dividend was paid, not when it was announced.
- Even if the price of the shares you own has risen, you do not have to pay tax on the profit until you sell the shares. Remember, however, that you will eventually have to pay tax unless the shares are held in an ISA or the profit is below your annual capital gains tax exemption.

MAKING CAPITAL GAINS

When you sell an investment at a higher price than you paid for it, you have made a capital gain. Your capital gain is the difference between what you originally paid and what you received when you sold it, minus any commissions. The tax you will pay depends on how long you owned the investment, and other factors. Ask your tax adviser for advice.

ASSESSING TYPES OF TAXABLE INCOME

Dividends that are interest. Some distributions commonly called dividends are actually interest. You must report these so-called dividends as interest on deposits.
Money market funds. Earnings from money market funds are taxable dividend income. Money market funds are a type of investment fund. Bank money market accounts, however, pay interest.
Interest on annuities. The accumulated interest on an annuity contract you sell before its maturity date is taxable.
Dividends on shares sold. If you sell shares of a company after the dividend is declared but before it is paid, you will still receive the dividend and must include it as taxable income.
Interest on deposit accounts. Most deposit accounts pay interest after having deducted the basic rate of tax. However, some accounts pay interest without deducting tax. This can be convenient for non-taxpayers and can help build interest more quickly because of the compounding effect.

33 You are liable for capital gains tax on shares only when you sell them.

34 Non-taxpayers can ask building societies and banks to pay interest without deducting tax.

DEDUCTING YOUR CAPITAL LOSSES

If your losses exceed your gains for the year, you may be able to deduct some or all of those capital losses against your ordinary income and offset them against any capital gains you have, thereby avoiding tax on those gains. You may also be able to carry capital losses forward to future years. Ask your tax adviser for details, because each situation is different. The responsibility, however, is on you to tell the Inland Revenue that you have made a loss and that you wish to carry it forward to use to balance against other profits made in other years.

STARTING OUT WITH CONFIDENCE

Knowing where to go and who to ask for help when you need it can actually make the investment process easier and may make it more profitable for you.

RECRUITING HELPERS

Think of investing your money as your business. You are creating wealth for yourself. You are the boss of your money. All the people involved in the business work for you.

35 Find people who give you the feeling that they truly understand your goals and your limitations.

DIRECTING PEOPLE TO WORK FOR YOU

As the one in charge of creating wealth for yourself, you have to direct the people you have hired. If you know what you want – if you have clearly established goals – you will have an easier time. The clearer you are about what you want, the easier it will be to pick the right people to help you and direct them accordingly. They will also be able to do a better job to help you get where you want to be.

SPOTTING TELLTALE SIGNS

A person who tries to steer you forcefully to a particular financial product as a planning solution or who regularly tries to sell you something instead of listening to your needs may not be the right financial adviser. In other words, an employee who has his or her own interests at heart rather than yours may not be the right employee for your business of creating wealth.

CHOOSING YOUR FINANCIAL ADVISER

A financial adviser can be an adviser at the highest level of your business. This person can help you think through your dreams for the future and the goals you want to achieve. Your adviser can also help you decide what other assistance you might need and help you select other professionals to fill those roles.

In order to understand what you want your money to do for you, and what choices are acceptable or unacceptable, your financial adviser may become a confidant in intimate aspects of your life. Therefore, it is important to select someone you trust and who has solid training in financial planning – not merely in selling investment products.

Financial advisers are paid a fee for their service or commission on the products that they sell. If a financial adviser is tied to a particular company, he or she may not be able to offer you every product and may try to sell you something from a limited range only, so try consulting an independent financial adviser to enable you to shop around.

FULL-SERVICE BROKERS	Full-service brokerage firms vary in what they charge you. As well as buying and selling on your behalf, they can offer advice and research about the companies in which you wish to invest.
DISCOUNT BROKERS	These firms can buy and sell on your behalf but do not offer advice. Fees tend to be lower than at other firms that offer a full advisory service.
INVESTMENT FUNDS	These funds pool the financial resources of many people to invest in a broad range of shares and bonds. By spreading the money over a number of different investments, they also hope to spread the risk. However, these funds also charge a fee.
BANKS	All banks offer investments that are aimed at protecting your money. Some offer brokerage services. Be aware that investment funds through a bank are no safer than those bought through a brokerage firm.
FINANCIAL ADVISERS	Financial advisers help you manage your investments. You pay either an annual fee or commission based on the value of your account.
ON-LINE BROKERS	On-line brokers can provide information instantly at any hour, with high interactivity and low commissions. Orders are not necessarily completed faster than through traditional brokers despite the common perception. While uncommon, computer malfunctions could be potentially troublesome.

PROTECTING YOURSELF

The financial industry is highly regulated, but your best protection is always to ask questions and be as well informed as you can. There are also many rules in place to protect you, and procedures to supervise those rules and assist you when necessary.

USING THE FINANCIAL SERVICES AUTHORITY

The Financial Services Authority (FSA) is the single statutory regulator responsible for regulating deposit-taking, insurance, and investment business. It is also responsible for tackling market abuse, promoting public understanding of the financial system, and reducing financial crime. It is a very powerful regulatory body and can provide enormous protection to investors and savers. However, if you have a complaint about a financial company, it is usually necessary to go through the company's complaints procedure first before taking your complaint to the FSA.

The FSA has four main objectives:

- To maintain market confidence.
- To promote public understanding of the financial system.
- To make sure that consumers are protected.
- To reduce the extent and effects of financial crime.

36 Always put your complaints in writing and keep detailed records.

CONSULTING THE FSA

The FSA offers consumers advice on how to deal with the financial services industry. Although it cannot advise on which investments are best for you, its consumer advice department has a wide range of information, which can clarify how the industry works. FSA Consumer Helpline: 0845 606 1234.

ENFORCING THE RULES

The Financial Services Authority can discipline authorized firms that have broken its rules. It can also bring a criminal prosecution against those who engage in regulated activities without authorization.

Among other things it can:

- Withdraw a firm's authorization.
- Discipline firms and people through public statements and financial penalties.
- Impose penalties for market abuse.
- Seek injunctions.
- Prosecute various offences.
- Require the return of money in order to compensate consumers.

37 Financial companies should try to resolve your written complaints within two months.

MAKING A COMPLAINT

If you have a complaint about a financial company, generally you should contact that company first and ask about its complaints procedure. Complain in writing and keep copies of all your letters. Do not part with any letters from the company without first taking a copy. You should also keep notes of any telephone conversations, including details of who you spoke with, which could prove invaluable later on if the complaint is not handled to your satisfaction. If you have exhausted the internal complaints procedure, or feel that you are being ignored, then you should complain via an independent complaints scheme. Ask the company which scheme it belongs to or, if necessary, call the FSA.

38 Many websites provide guidance for investors concerned about fraudulent practices.

READING A STATEMENT

Once you have chosen your investments, you should receive regular statements of your accounts. Statements vary depending on the institution, but in general you will find the following information listed on your monthly statement.

CHECKING YOUR WEALTH

An account statement gives you a snapshot of how your share portfolio is performing. It will tell you not only which shares you own, but how much you bought them for, and what they were worth when the account statement was issued. Since there is so much information in the statement, it also provides you with an instant wealth check. You can ascertain whether you are making or losing money and how well or badly your investments are doing.

CALCULATING PROFITS AND TAX

Your account statement will give you a fairly good idea of whether you will have to pay tax and how much you might have to pay. The statement itself is unlikely to refer to tax specifically, but the information it provides will help you work it out for yourself. Share-based investments can be taxed in two ways: through income tax and capital gains tax. One of the biggest problems most people face in trying to work out how much capital gains tax they will have to pay is working out the profit they have made on any specific share over many years. To calculate the figure, they need to know the purchase and sale prices of the share. Since many people lose the original paperwork, this can be very difficult. You should therefore keep all your account statements and all paperwork relating to purchases and sales.

◀**KEEPING STATEMENTS**
Keep hold of your statements, and file them. They are useful for tax planning, investment planning, and even inheritance tax planning.

SAMPLE PORTFOLIO VALUATION

Ms J Smith
Rose Cottage
Small Village
ANYTOWN
WX1 2YZ

Portfolio ref: 1234
Page: 1
FTSE 100 5229.12
FTSE ALL SHARE 2539.69

These are the values of the main stock-market indices at the time of the valuation report.

The FTSE 100, FT All Share and Mid-market prices are taken at the end of business on 10 April

Quantity	Name/Description of Security/Shares	Purchase Cost (£)	Mid-market Price (£)	Mid-market Value (£)	Gross Income (£)	Gross Yield (%)
	OIL & GAS					
6000.00	ANY CO PETROLEUM GBP0.01	315.00	0.032500	195.00		
	GENERAL RETAILERS					
1730.00	ANY RETAIL GROUP ORD GBP0.01	500.00	0.055000	95.15		
	LEISURE, ENTERTAINMENT & HOTELS					
7499.00	ANY SPORT PLC ORD GBP0.05	1,303.00	0.147500	1,106.10		
	SPECIALITY & OTHER FINANCE					
30552.00	ANY FINANCE GROUP ORD GBP0.01	1,001.05	0.001400	42.77		
1500.00	ANY FINANCE GROUP WTS(SUB FOR ORD)	3.00	0.007900	11.85		
	PORTFOLIO TOTAL	3,122.05		1,450.87	0.00	0.00

This column reflects the value of the dividend as a percentage of the share price.

This shows you the value of the dividends paid by the shares.

This figure shows the total value of your holding in those shares.

This column shows the amount of shares you currently own in each company.

This column shows the sectors in which you have invested, the name of each company, and the type of share bought.

This shows the total portfolio value at the time when the report was compiled.

This column shows an indicative price halfway between the purchase price and the sale price.

USING YOUR STATEMENT TO MONITOR PERFORMANCE

Account statements are invaluable for providing essential information at a glance. In particular, they let you know the following important details:

- How well your account was doing when it was opened.
- How well your account was doing when the report was compiled.
- What assets you own – or, more precisely, what assets you had in your account at the close of the period.

INDEX

ACKNOWLEDGMENTS

AUTHOR'S ACKNOWLEDGMENTS

The production of this book has called on the skills of many people. Marc Robinson would like particularly to mention the editors at Dorling Kindersley, and consultant Nick Clemente. He wishes to dedicate this book to Bert and Phoebe Robinson for their unending encouragement and to Zachary Robinson for his great patience and support when it was most needed.

PUBLISHER'S ACKNOWLEDGMENTS

Dorling Kindersley would like to give special thanks to Sarah Pennells for her invaluable advice and assistance. The publisher would also like to thank everyone who generously lent props for the photoshoots, and the following for their help and participation:

Editorial Stephanie Rubenstein; **Jacket Editor** Jane Oliver-Jedrzejak; **Design and Layout** Hedayat Sandjari; Isabel de Cordova; **Picture researchers** Mark Dennis; Sam Ruston; **Jacket Designer** John Dinsdale; **Preflighting** Mark Schroeder; **Consultants** Nick Clemente; Skeeter; **Indexer** Indexing Specialists; **Proofreader** Caroline Curtis; **Photography** Anthony Nex; **Photographers' assistants** Victor Boghassian; Stephanie Fowler; **Models** Sandy Crozier; Victor Boghassian; **Special thanks to** Teresa Clavasquin for her generous support and assistance.

AUTHORS' BIOGRAPHIES

Adam Shaw presents BBC1's daily financial programme *Working Lunch*. He is also the author of *Political Rhubarb* and co-author of *Money and How to Make More of It*. He has presented *Business Breakfast* and *Financial World Tonight*. He has also reported from Japan, USA, Canada, and France.

Marc Robinson is a founding director of LEAP (Latino Education Achievement Project), a non-profit organization dedicated to empowering Latinos to be more informed, confident, and active participants in the US. He is also co-founder of Internet-based moneytours.com, a personal finance resource for corporations, universities, credit unions, and other institutions interested in helping their constituents make intelligent decisions about their financial lives. He is the author of the KISS guide on Personal Finance. He wrote the original *The Wall Street Journal Guide to Understanding Money and Markets* and co-published a personal finance series with Time Life Books. He wrote a children's book about onomatopoeia in different languages, and has produced coffee table books for *The Wall Street Journal* to commemorate its 100th anniversary, and for NBC to commemorate its 75th anniversary. In his two decades in the financial services industry, Marc has provided marketing consulting to many top Wall Street firms. He is admitted to practise law in New York State.

PICTURE CREDITS

Key: *a* above, *b* bottom, *c* centre, *l* left, *r* right, *t* top
Corbis: Jose Luis Palaez, Inc. 4c; **Getty Images:** Jonathan Kim 9bl.

The information contained in this publication is general in nature and is not intended to provide advice, guidance, or expertise of any nature regarding financial or investment decisions. Neither Dorling Kindersley nor any of its authors or contributors make any representations or warranties with respect to the professional experience or credentials of the authors or contributors, or to the merits of the information or materials contained herein. The reader should consult independent financial advisers and investment professionals prior to making any decision or plan.